AGAINST

THE FALLING EVIL

AGAINST
THE FALLING EVIL

James McMichael

THE SWALLOW PRESS INC.

CHICAGO

Published by

The Swallow Press Incorporated
1139 South Wabash Avenue
Chicago, Illinois 60605

ISBN 0-8040-0552-4
LIBRARY OF CONGRESS CATALOG NO. 72-171878

New Poetry Series Volume No. 43

Acknowledgements:

Grateful acknowledgment is made to the following publications in
which some of these poems first appeared: *The Iowa Review, Pequod,
The Southern Review,* and *The West Coast Review.*

"The Vegetables" first appeared in *Poetry.*

to the memory of my father;
for Bobby and Geoff

CONTENTS

IV   The Circus Monologues

V

I

Janet

All the bakeries have closed.
The women of the bakeries
Must find something to do.
They clean the sidewalks
Until the sidewalks are as clean
As the floors of bakeries.

They go into the homes of the sick.
They go into the elevators.
With their good smells, they go
Into the parks, and everyone
Follows them there. No one is left
To be sad or talk of harm.
There are flowers, and candles,
And over their own singing

They hear her coming to them
Like a flood of moths, a powder
Of small wings, and she settles
Everywhere, on all faces,
Janet, her heart opening.

Lumberbarks

No one is here
To tell the boats not to think of wood.
It is winter
And everyone is inside.

The wood is outside.
It is on the docks,
And the docks are of wood.
The sawmills and warehouses
Are of wood. There is wood
In the trees, and the trees are outside.

The snow has made everything very still.
The water does not rock the boats at all
And they think nothing of their moorings.
They will go among the trees.

They move away from the docks,
Going alone
Either up the sound, or down.

There is much fog.
They do not find the rivers easily.
Their rigging is stiff with frost
And they hope soon to feel their decks buckle,
Their masts and spars bloom with a thousand cones.

The Assassin

He is what you have thrown away:
The old light bulbs, jars, windows,
But mostly shelves. The shelves
Are very full. He does not want

Anything to touch anything else.
He sees that there is much crowding.
Colored bottles are rubbing
Figurines of ships and swans;

As if it were wine, the light
Spills into the stems of glasses.
There is no help for it.
He must touch each piece himself,

Must nudge it toward its fall,
Trusting that it will not break,
Will not come down, that it will
Like where it finds itself.

The Cabin North of It All

You build it where you will be heard only by chance
And at a great distance. The hammer is moss

And the saw moves like the wolf's shoulder,
Smoothly, and with no sound. It is a good start.

The seasons themselves come singly, and you are still
North of it all, north of brooding on that later time

When it will be quieter, when the door will not hold,
When the raccoons, on their first night inside,

Will not trouble to be afraid, their heads
Bent in the squares of moonlight, dreaming of the north.

The Silk Smith

His hands are not together,
But you think of them that way.
They are the cocoon.
Inside, all the threads are pulsing.
He worries the knuckles into fires.

You have brought him
Whatever you would have him touch.
You hope he will bless it,
Will make it fine and strong,

Will make for it a place where no one dies,
Where no one whispers that anyone
Is dying. He can do this, you tell him,
And he seems to hear you,
For you see that his hands

Are not together. They are at his sides.
You can see the backs of them.
You have watched him for a long time.
His hands are at his sides.

Throwing Down Gulls

They dribble an oily silt
And suck their heads into their necks,
Shifting from foot to foot,
Slipping a little in the slick
Droppings on their perches.

For days I have waited to see them
Rise onto their legs, open
And lift heavily into the sky.
The few I take in my net
And carry to the cliff and throw

Down, catch in their fall,
Catch and pull up into an easy
Glide, an easy pumping,
The echoes of their screams
Piping through the high basins.

What He Hears

His face is undressed,
Ready to be prayed for.
He is very tired
But listens for the whisper
Of those who miss him.
What he hears is old,
Is at home in damp places
And trails its spittle
Over cold leaves and stones.
Camphor leaks from its lips.
It has nothing to say.

The Conjurer of Waters

I cool the ankles
Of the dustiest Conquistador.
I am his leisure to conjure
Gold, grassy esplanades,
Grand cities of water.

I am the high lakes.
The rocks around me are clean and terrible.
I tender the sides of clear-eyed fishes
As if I were air.

I am the clouds and will not come down.

Sleeping In Your Prayer-Cloth

Weave into it the likeness
Of forts or sage or cowtowns or
Whatever charms will make it easier to lie down
Years before you were born.
Bind yourself in it
As if it were your only clothing.
When you want to move begin with your arms.
Spread them and feel the seams
Stretch whitely, full of wolves.
The trails are not marked
Nor does your cloth tell you where you are.
You carry wood and travel only by day.
With each shallow fording your blood
Stuns into forgetfulness.
Your eyes are hail-stones,
You murmur about ascents and passes
And follow yourself slowly in narrowing circles, settle
Quietly like snow.
This is your penance.
This is for watching yourself sleep.

II

THE VEGETABLES

E.L.M., 1900-1951

The Artichoke

She bore only the heart,
Worked at the stem with her
Fingers, pulling it to her,
And into her, like a cord.

She would sustain him,
Would cover his heart.
The hairy needles
And the bigger leaves,

These she licked into shape,
Tipping each with its point.
He is the mud-flower,
The thorny hugger.

The Asparagus

She sent packs of great beasts to pass
Over him, trailing belly-fur and dust,
Bending their nostrils to his frail spear.
This was to toughen him. For what?
Stupidly, like a squirrel, standing up,
Looking here and there, looking to all sides,

He is cut down and taken away.
She can smell him steaming, his crowns
Already tender, his spine giving in.
Now he is threatening to wither terribly,
And slip from the water altogether,
And billow through the kitchen like prayer.

15

The Cauliflower

Her words clot in his head.
He presses himself to remember
And feels the skin peel back,
The skull bleach, crack, fall away.

All that's left of him is the brain,
Its tissue knotting up to shade him,
The pain of its light pulsing
How to move, how to move.

Herbs

Before fog leaves the scrub-oak
Or the grasses of the downland,
Take dragonwort under the black alder,
Take cockspur grass and henbane,
The belladonna, the deadly nightshade.
Free them as you would a spider's web,
Singing over them: Out, little wen,
                    Out, little wen.
Sing this into the mouth of the woman.

16

Corn

I am the corn quail.
What I do is quick.
You will know only
The muffled clucking,
The scurry, the first
Shiver of feathers
And I will be up,
I will be in your
Head with no way out,
Wings beating at the
Air behind your eyes.

Celery

The hope with
water is that it
will conceal nothing,

that a clearness
will follow upon it
like the clearness
after much rain,

or the clearness
where the air
reaches to the river
and touches it,

where the rain
falls from the trees
into the river.

17

Bell Pepper

To find enough rooms for the gathering
The walls go on alone not waiting
For corners but thinking of sleeves
And how the wind fills them and the snow
Fills them and how cold it is without
Fires when there are not enough rooms.

Potatoes

It had been growing in her like vegetables.
She was going into the ground where it could
Do better, where she could have potatoes.

They would be small and easily mistaken
For stones. It would fall to her to
Sort them out, persuade them to stay

Close to her, comforting her, letting her
Wear them on her body, in her hair,
Helping her hold always very still.

18

III

The Operation

The Child

These are my doctors. They say:
"It is time to go to sleep."
They give me something.

I close my eyes.   *In order to*
I try to open my eyes.   *produce a*
They start to cut me.   *chemical lesion*
It hurts.   *of the reticular*
                                    activating
They talk about cutting   *system,*
Others they cut.

They take something out of me.
This is like a fire.
I think it is my mother.

21

The Pain

There were the blue edges
Of the iceberg. Ships had to be
Very careful of them.
He would have to be careful

Of teeth. Babies are not
Born with teeth. They might
Eat themselves. To stay awake
He would just lick his fingers.

*the volume of
nitrous oxide
must equal or
exceed the res-
piratory volume.
It did not.*

The Others

We are the names of our fathers:
Beckwith, Bergendahl, Collis.

There is nothing for us to do.

We have begun to sleep
Beyond our faces. We are

Sleeping into the tails of cats,
Tails that don't remember fur.

Already, the waters are
Sleeping into us. Like twilight,
We are on the wind. We are

What you hear when you're afraid.

Ataraxia, sedation, narcosis, anesthesia, and complete medulary depression were apparent but unrealized. The patient remained immobilized, awake.

Going Down

At first, those who noticed spoke mostly
Of my naivete. They insisted I was
Like the five-year-old boy on the beach,
Digging his way down and into China.

They speculated that I had left
Something behind me in my late infancy,
And that I was just now about the business
Of going after it. I was advised

That to be taken seriously,
I must research the earth's composition,
Choosing with great care tools, food, clothes.
They assured me it was a long way through.

The angle of the cut, too, was essential.
Did I indeed want to end up in China?
They admitted they were very much
Charmed by my poise, by what seemed almost,

At times, my boredom. And after I unearthed
Three soft-shell crabs in my first handful of sand,
And dug some more, and lowered myself
Down through the first few feet of the damp grains,

I heard them promise that they would shield
The mouth of the shaft from the tide. And they did.
Looking up, I could see them in their huddle,
And above them all, that blue vacancy,

Until night. Even then they watched, called to me,
And cared. Weeks later, the authorities came.
They wanted answers, and were told that no one,
No one had been fooled by my strategies.

American Album

Ahab's Children

It was no ivory leg
By which they were begotten.
It is not incidental to them
That they are not thought well of;
That God, with a charm
Singularly His own,
Had christened them heretics.
Pray for them
As you watch them burn.
Pray that their loins might hold
No colder luck for their own.

1880: Custer County, Nebraska

The camera is you, and he poses
As if you are even now his woman.

He is asking what you will do for him.
It will not be enough to imagine

Caring for him at the end, feeling
The eyes gone cold as you close the lids.

You must be there for him when he is strong,
Covering his body with your own,

Taking on and into you the full
Explosions of his breath and seed.

Grandmother

She knew the
sound of waiting
for the first birds

of morning,
walked out early
into that sound
of no sound

and brushed the angel
tipping the shredded
palm-fronds,
the drops of fog.

1892: Charles R. Savage, Salt Lake City, Utah

To be old, and home, and waiting for
One's children and one's Christmas dinner
Is to sit at the window and not look out.

It is to know that what matters
Is the waiting; that in this City,
And at such a time, one does well

To wait anywhere: in upstairs bedrooms
Where the snow-laden lattice of the arbor
Leans against the casements; in kitchens

Busy with smells, Sisters, and much worrying.
One can wait even in the cellars
Of the coldest houses, giving oneself

To the promise of births, millions of them,
And of the millions of rebirths in the pools
Of mountain rivers sluggish with ice.

Report

The children do not go out
But spend whole days at their maps.
Their mothers catch them in lies
About their grandfather's scars,
Overhear them speak of the
Sioux and Crow, the Cheyenne,
Nez Perce and Assiniboin,
Men with the eyes of zebra
Running before the lions.
They tell of them caught and down,
The unfolding of their flanks,
Of brains pouring from their ears
In puddles that bleach, dry there
And rise, shattering like light
Against the teeth of animals.

Wing

1.

Rolling, he is rolled from sleep
Slightly, and slightly, until
He doesn't know if the quake
And what it wakes are his dream.

He guesses what it's about,
Guesses the whole history
Of the world and how it once
Was level: plains and grasses,

Pools, rivers that flowed, not down,
But by their own wills to seas
Final in the sun, and full.
It is as if his waking

Courses through the wind, as if
Soundlessly, from special wells
Deeper than his blood he feels
The first urgings of the tides.

It is too late not to move,
Knowing that to move is to
Bring on quakes, heavings of soil,
The long peaks, slopes and trenches.

2.

He remembers yesterday.
Through sage, lupine, and the dry
Forests of fir and hemlock,
The slow pull up the moraine;

Remembers noon, timberline,
The granite crest and the cool
Wonder of its white banners.
He had eaten from those drifts.

But then there had been the lake.
Submerged in its green shallows
Was what he had not come for,
What no one yet had come for.

He hadn't mistaken it.
It was nose-down and intact,
Its tail only a few feet
Under the glassy cover.

He thought of its people, how
Wherever they were headed,
The world was again for them
Flat, altogether perfect.

3.

Above him are the pines, boughs
Brimming with a frost of stars,
The sky streaked from time to time
By the white traces of worlds

Falling everywhere. But theirs
Is not the quake he wakes to.
It is the plane's, rehearsing
Again and again for him

Its last landing in the lake,
Each time missing, just missing
Clearing the ridge. Then its plunge.
After eight tries its people

Are not hopeful, call to him:
"Come up to us, meet us here,
In the air, where it is safe."
He declines, and it goes on

Framed in a great pile of cloud,
Full-bellied, its feathers preened,
Now banking with the terrain,
Steady, stopping for no one.

IV

THE CIRCUS MONOLOGUES

Barker

Grain elevators in the Dakotas
Are tipping to their sides,
Spilling over Nebraska, and Kansas,
And south, even to the Gulf.
The Florida Keys are drifting toward Cuba.
In What Cheer, Iowa
And Adulation, Montana
Everyone is holding on for dear life.

Fat Man

So that I might include all things
I propose a certain

Bodily enlargement and begin to look
Rather unlike myself.

As I remember, it starts
Somewhere in the lower calf.

I sense, as I pull it on,
That the elastic in my left

Sock will no longer do.
I may be growing fat.

It may be that simple.
Look at me. Is it cancer?

Hermaphrodite

I see a mad girl. She has to be watched.
As they lead her toward the swings
She knows they want her to cross the grass
And she sees it rigid and silver, like forks.
Already she can feel it at her ankles,
Feel it higher, growing, trying to get
Inside her, into her fever.
She whispers that she doesn't want the grass,
But they know best. And then she is over it,
Pleading "What can I do? What can I do?"
It seems a fair question.

The answer is that, like all of us,
She can just wait. The fever
Will one day leave through her bowels.
They will bury it and she will do
A little dance: a new dance this time,
Nothing at all like her old dances.
Why I love her is that her tightest folds
Will open only to me, open only slightly,
And having been closed so long will love me,
Will love what I have waited to give, I,
Who haven't half enough for you.

Clown

They are anxious to get on with it
And question me at once about my diffidence.
What turds am I hiding in my mouth?
They tell me that I appear to be a burp,

That my walk and my whole demeanor
Have the drift of a deflated mother blimp.
They look for slots along my underside,
Fingering the several creases they find,

Puzzling over the flaps. Are they operative?
I assure them they are and begin to inflate.
They say they haven't room for that in here.
I see that they are content to watch.

I fill the near and now the far
Corners of the ceiling and the floor,
Overturning pitchers of water, name plates,
Odd chairs, ashtrays, a stenographer.

It is suggested that they should puncture me.
They would be as generous as possible,
Would fold me here and there, hand me to myself,
And send me home so that I might rest.

But no one moves. Nor do they even
Glance at one another. Now I am ready:
The flaps open, the hooks extend, and I
Take them in. I drag through the window, out.

And away! We pass over kites, steeples,
Smokestacks, ascending baseballs, water towers,
Weathervanes, skylights, gazebos, outdoor clocks.
Inside, I give them a weather of much noise.

The thunder rattles around my ribs.
They complain of not being able to sleep.
They lie down in the beds of their children.
It is no quieter there but the counterpanes

Are thick and quilted, and they pull them up
Just under their noses. They wish the pillows
Didn't smell so much of sons and daughters
And feel in the warm imprint of those skulls

The glory of the lightning to small eyes.
With the calm they are less restive, but awake.
It is dark, in mid-summer, and from their beds
They know again what it is to want to play.

They hear spoons and sherbet on the patio.
Their cats are high in the chinese elm.
They think of a blimp chartered by themselves,
Touring the city, and filled with animals.

Cannon

We might at this time project
That among the forthcoming assassinations
There will be one of especial purity.
Think with me for a moment of the tool.
You know already, of course, its clean
Tumescence, its charge, and can calculate from these
The surety of its thrust. But what promises more still
Is that it need never be inserted.
The mother-to-be, virgin and unaware,
Simply awaits in her turn the immaculate
Insemination. And think of her births.

Ringmaster

Regarding the survivors:
They will at all times be shown
The highest of courtesies.

Direct them to the windows.
The swirls of algae and thick
Streamers of moss, the very
Pressure, too, of the water—
These should persuade them that there
Is nowhere, really, to go.

Admit that the horn is dull,
That, indeed, at this wet depth
It will be of little use,
And that in the search for them
The salvage crew will rely
Rather on the two headlights.
They will want to sing of these.
You will provide metaphors.

Speak of the two beams as swaths,
Or candles, or wings of quail.
Tell them the light will carry
Beyond the surface, into
The low rain, into the trees.

Tell them the light will be seen.
Tell them they will not be lost.
You will trust us to save you.
With all deliberate speed.

From the High-wire

I am dropped from above.
In my glide, I gather myself
For the touch of the wire,
The balance.

To much applause
I pivot on the point of a single toe
And take requests.

They ask for a dream.

I dream of balloons,
Red ones, fibrous, moist.

I put my hand in my mouth.
I reach down as far as I can.

I find a lung and pull it out gently.
It hangs from my lip like a great tongue
And lolls, wags, wants coaxing.
I stroke it.
I teach it to breathe like a bird.

V

Letter

I write to you of what seems to me
Distinct progress. It has been some time
Since my prospects have been so little
Ingrown; since my simplest of activities,

Like waking, have been untroubled by the dream.
You know already it was a dream of sleep,
My own sleep, a sleep as isolate as the poles,
Basic, and invisible. To say it is gone

Is not to say that now, the moment of waking
Is to think first of poplars stretching
Above the steep eaves. It is to say

That this morning, here, I thought first
Of being awake; that now, in me, the sun
Stirs like my own liver, rich with blood.

In the Middle of the Day, Among Friends

That it wasn't good for him was clear
Mostly from what he didn't think.
In the middle of the day, among friends,
He thought of it raining for many days,

Of reading in his bath while it rained;
Thought of the window open, the cold air
Moving over his lids and chin.
He thought of the rain,

The trees between his house and the next,
The walk in the rain between here and there.
If he didn't think that he would take the walk
It was because his bath was warm, because

The walk was too much like itself,
Too little like his bath. And the trees:
If he didn't think of them naked,
Stretching in the rain; if he didn't think

Of what they pushed up, what they pushed through,
Of the dark, close, crouch of the night on them there,
It was because it wasn't good for him,
Because he knew it wasn't good for him.

Thinking of the Oregon Rains

Wishing seasons through this haze
I imagine a grand
Preponderance of water:
Scotch broom and fern bowing
Heavily toward the first fall run,
Whorled gutters and their limber bark-flakes,
Steam rising from the road
And from the chimneys
Wisps of still another gray.
What are my sins in all this weather?
Accident is my substance.
Oblique remonstrances whip
Windward into rain,
Fear settles into sounds
As death, driest of rain forests,
Steals nothing of the velvet dampness.
And staying these changes,
Only the remembrances—
Remembrances
Of earlier severance from evil,
Of constancy, remorseless good,
And of the loneliness therewith.

Lady Good

It had to be said about her
That she was good, got better still,
And that when he left her, or died,
Or did whatever worse he could
Do to her, that she took it on;
Took on not what he did to her
But what it did to him to do it.

Christmas Elegy –
Bodie, California

Was it here you hunted?
Below me by half a hill
A buck noses through the freezing powder,
Careless of history,
Of you or me.

Behind his foraging eyes
He knows the nothing that you now know,
A totality of seasons and temperatures
Undisturbed
By winter night fantasies
Of jade light throbbing to the north.

He encounters only instance,
Sterile as the snowscape,
Safe
From imagining that last
Tumble out of time.

Which of us, hunter,
Should move away through these hills,
Looking toward the slow, alluvial
Swell of the Sierra?
Which of us should climb the crest of the icy cirque,
Guess the inland meadow grasses,
And prophesy a thaw?

Quicker, even, than deceit,
These sixty winters severing us dissolve
And I am cold.

The Last Distances

The first distances
Were cultivated, proper.

With them I watched you
For fine difference

And there was none. Now,
Inebriate with lesion,

I ignore as I can
The subtleties of withdrawal.

It is no longer careful,
This making you a stranger.

Just Lying There

The rocks on my roof
Thud to the owl's dull shuffle.
He does not care
That I tell you why I do not sleep;
About a night
Long, there, beyond him,
Long
And sumptuous with stars
That measure in their going
Neither mind nor cold.
Nor need you, if you care, be told
The anarchy of dream,
Of sleep itself,
Of the last owl.

A Passion

Waking,
I remembered summer afternoons,
Our path
Tunneled in eucalyptus
And a softness of sun.
Soon there were sycamores,
Their leaves
Ferreting,
Cool,
Through the culverts,
The shallows of the last rain.
What there had been of you
In this last sustenance
I had not asked.
Nor did I wonder this evening,
Wading through riffles,
Scattering fingerling from the head of pools,
Waiting into the darkness
For the last gestures of the trout.
It is only now—
Hours before the next light,
As I see the slow, circling
Shadow of an owl
On a thicket of aspen silvering the moon,
And think
Deeper, into the pines, across the creek,
Of wild foxglove,
Its stalks
Spiked with a purple
Still darker than time—
It is only now that you become
Some tameless emissary
Of grace.

From the
Quiet Suburb

Higher, in the lodgepole, red
Columbine is a month gone.

Even below the passes
The cold is now coming on.

But there it is easier,
The cold. Its artists of despair,

Its Donners, measure a brilliance
Glacial in its bald coming.

Here in this limp dusk, I think:
I'm neither ready, nor not.

Chest Pains

1.

From these constrictions of flesh
There is to be no reprieve.
And as they grip it
I feel in the golden
Thump-pumping muscle
The longevity of a cabbage.
It is to want to know what to do
When the rivers for the last time freeze.
It is to want to be
The Bear Who Could Do Anything.

2.

It was when they asked him
Was there anything he couldn't do
That the Bear brought his press conference
Smartly to a close and caught the bus.
On his subsequent history—if it be that—
We can of course only speculate.

If he had been seen
Circuiting the deserts and prairies
Agallop on the ten-league
Strides of his wild sorrel,
Homing, always, to the alpenglow
Of the Wasatch, Wind River
And Absaroka Ranges,
Would it have mattered

That one night he turned not altogether
Politely in his sleep, that his lids
Kicked open to his pulse and his eyes
Flashed into the freeze?
For it may be
That he did pass through the low air,
Ascending to his celestial
Template in the Northern Constellation,
Fixing his fur with a resonance of fire.

Imagine him there with your children.